Your Government:
How It Works

The Supreme
Court

Kay Cornelius

Arthur M. Schlesinger, jr.
Senior Consulting Editor

Chelsea House Publishers
Philadelphia

CHELSEA HOUSE PUBLISHERS
Editor in Chief Stephen Reginald
Production Manager Pamela Loos
Art Director Sara Davis
Director of Photography Judy L. Hasday
Managing Editor James D. Gallagher
Senior Production Editor LeeAnne Gelletly

Staff for THE SUPREME COURT
Project Editor/Publishing Coordinator Jim McAvoy
Associate Art Director Takeshi Takahashi
Series Designer Takeshi Takahashi, Keith Trego

The Chelsea House World Wide Web address is
http://www.chelseahouse.com

3 5 7 9 8 6 4 2

Library of Congress Cataloging-in-Publication Data

Cornelius, Kay.
    The Supreme Court / by Kay Cornelius.
        p. cm. — (Your government—how it works)
    Includes bibliographical references and index.
    Summary: Surveys the history, decisions, justices, and contro-
versies of the highest court in the land.
    ISBN 0-7910-5532-9 (hc)
    1. United States. Supreme Court—Juvenile literature. 2. Judicial
power—United States—Juvenile literature. [1. United States.
Supreme Court. 2. Courts. 3. Law.] I. Title. II. Series.
KF8742.Z9 C59 2000
347.73'26—dc21   99-048457

Contents

YOUR GOVERNMENT
HOW IT WORKS

The Central Intelligence Agency

The Federal Bureau of Investigation

The History of the Democratic Party

The History of the Republican Party

The History of Third Parties

The House of Representatives

How a Bill Is Passed

How to Become an Elected Official

The Impeachment Process

The Presidency

The Senate

The Supreme Court

Introduction

Government: Crises of Confidence

Arthur M. Schlesinger, jr.

FROM THE START, Americans have regarded their government with a mixture of reliance and mistrust. The men who founded the republic understood the importance of government. "If men were angels," observed the 51st Federalist Paper, "no government would be necessary." But men are not angels. Because human beings are subject to wicked as well as to noble impulses, government was deemed essential to assure freedom and order.

The American revolutionaries, however, also knew that government could become a source of injury and oppression. The men who gathered in Philadelphia in 1787 to write the Constitution therefore had two purposes in mind: They wanted to establish a strong central authority and to limit that central authority's capacity to abuse its power.

To prevent the abuse of power, the Founding Fathers wrote two basic principles into the Constitution. The principle of federalism divided power between the state governments and the central authority. The principle of the separation of powers subdivided the central authority itself into three branches—the executive, the legislative, and the judiciary—so that "each may be a check on the other."

YOUR GOVERNMENT: HOW IT WORKS examines some of the major parts of that central authority, the federal government. It explains how various officials, agencies, and departments operate and explores the political organizations that have grown up to serve the needs of government.

Introduction

The federal government as presented in the Constitution was more an idealistic construct than a practical administrative structure. It was barely functional when it came into being.

This was especially true of the executive branch. The Constitution did not describe the executive branch in any detail. After vesting executive power in the president, it assumed the existence of "executive departments" without specifying what these departments should be. Congress began defining their functions in 1789 by creating the Departments of State, Treasury, and War.

President Washington, assisted by Secretary of the Treasury Alexander Hamilton, equipped the infant republic with a working administrative structure. Congress also continued that process by creating more executive departments as they were needed.

Throughout the 19th century, the number of federal government workers increased at a consistently faster rate than did the population. Increasing concerns about the politicization of public service led to efforts—bitterly opposed by politicians—to reform it in the latter part of the century.

The 20th century saw considerable expansion of the federal establishment. More importantly, it saw growing impatience with bureaucracy in society as a whole.

The Great Depression during the 1930s confronted the nation with its greatest crisis since the Civil War. Under Franklin Roosevelt, the New Deal reshaped the federal government, assigning it a variety of new responsibilities and greatly expanding its regulatory functions. By 1940, the number of federal workers passed the 1 million mark.

Critics complained of big government and bureaucracy. Business owners resented federal regulation. Conservatives worried about the impact of paternalistic government on self-reliance, on community responsibility, and on economic and personal freedom.

When the United States entered World War II in 1941, government agencies focused their energies on supporting the war effort. By the end of World War II, federal civilian employment had risen to 3.8 million. With peace, the federal establishment declined to around 2 million in 1950. Then growth resumed, reaching 2.8 million by the 1980s.

A large part of this growth was the result of the national government assuming new functions such as: affirmative action in civil rights, environmental protection, and safety and health in the workplace.

Some critics became convinced that the national government was a steadily growing behemoth swallowing up the liberties of the people. The 1980s brought new intensity to the debate about government growth. Foes of Washington bureaucrats preferred local government, feeling it more responsive to popular needs.

But local government is characteristically the government of the locally powerful. Historically, the locally powerless have often won their human and constitutional rights by appealing to the national government. The national government has defended racial justice against local bigotry, upheld the Bill of Rights against local vigilantism, and protected natural resources from local greed. It has civilized industry and secured the rights of labor organizations. Had the states' rights creed prevailed, perhaps slavery would still exist in the United States.

Americans are still of two minds. When pollsters ask large, spacious questions—Do you think government has become too involved in your lives? Do you think government should stop regulating business?—a sizable majority opposes big government. But when asked specific questions about the practical work of government—Do you favor Social Security? Unemployment compensation? Medicare? Health and safety standards in factories? Environmental protection?—a sizable majority approves of intervention.

We do not like bureaucracy, but we cannot live without it. We need its genius for organizing the intricate details of our daily lives. Without bureaucracy, modern society would collapse. It would be impossible to run any of the large public and private organizations we depend on without bureaucracy's division of labor and hierarchy of authority. The challenge is to keep these necessary structures of our civilization flexible, efficient, and capable of innovation.

More than 200 years after the drafting of the Constitution, Americans still rely on government but also mistrust it. These attitudes continue to serve us well. What we mistrust, we are more likely to monitor. And government needs our constant attention if it is to avoid inefficiency, incompetence, and arbitrariness. Without our informed participation, it cannot serve us individually or help us as a people to attain the lofty goals of the Founding Fathers.

The Supreme Court Building, Washington, D.C. Decisions made here have the power to affect the lives of all Americans.

CHAPTER 1

The History of the Supreme Court

THE SUPREME COURT IS often called the highest court in the land because it has the last word in deciding how some important matters are to be settled. What the Supreme Court says has the power to make a big difference in the lives of all Americans, no matter their age or the color of their skin, or where they live. Its decisions, called rulings, are reported in newspapers and on radio and television news broadcasts.

We are used to hearing about the Supreme Court, yet few people know much about the history of the Court or what it really does. We might think that today's Supreme Court always existed, but that is not so. To see how the United States Supreme Court got started, we must travel more than 200 years back in time.

After the American colonies broke away from England and won the right to be an independent country, its people had to decide what kind of government they wanted. Would the United States of America have a king? What sorts of laws would it have? Who would make the laws? How would disagreements between people and states be decided?

To answer these questions, leaders from all the 13 former colonies of Great Britain came together to write the Constitution of the United States. This document begins with the words "We the people of the United States."

The Constitution spells out the rights and duties of the citizens and sets up the form of government that is still used today. It is called a living document because it was written over 200 years ago by men who could not know the kinds of problems America would face in the future. As a result, it has had over two dozen amendments, or extra rules, added over the years. The first 10 amendments were adopted in 1791. Known as the Bill of Rights, these additions to the Constitution name rights each citizen has and limit the power of the government over its people.

The Bill of Rights, adopted in 1791 and signed by Vice President John Adams, contains the first 10 amendments to the United States Constitution.

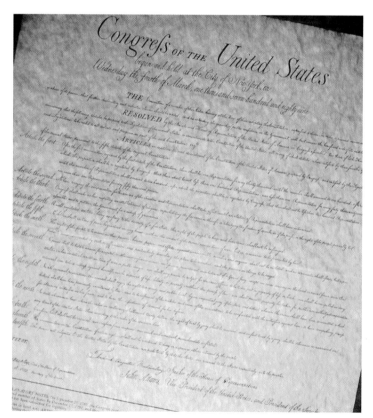

The Constitution calls for the United States government to have three departments, or branches, to carry out tasks. The power to govern the country is divided into three parts, so that no one branch will have too much power over the other two.

The executive branch is headed by the president, who is elected to serve for four years. He works and lives in the White House at 1600 Pennsylvania Avenue in Washington, D.C. The president is the commander in chief of the armed forces and must see that federal laws are carried out.

The legislative branch has two parts, the House of Representatives and the Senate. Together, they make up the United States Congress. Its members are elected and must live in the places they serve. Congress makes the laws and collects money to run the government through taxation. The members of Congress do their work in the United States Capitol building in Washington, D.C.

The judicial branch settles disputes. The word judicial comes from a Latin word meaning judge. The Constitution has quite a bit to say about the executive and legislative branches. However, it gives less information about the judicial branch.

Article III
The Judicial Department

Section 1. The judicial power of the United States, shall be vested in one Supreme Court, and in such inferior Courts as the Congress may from time to time ordain and establish. The judges, both of the Supreme and inferior Courts, shall hold their Offices during good Behaviour, and shall, at stated Times, receive for their Services, a Compensation, which shall not be diminished during their Continuance in Office.

The writers of the Constitution wanted to make sure that judges would be free to do their jobs without fear that they might not get paid if some official did not like the way they decided a case. Justices may keep their jobs for as long as they show "good behavior," so they cannot be fired without a reason.

Before Article III of the Constitution of the United States called for it to be created, there had never been anything quite like the United States Supreme Court. The Constitution was signed on September 17, 1787. The rules for making federal courts came two years later in the Judiciary Act of 1789. It set up a Supreme Court with a chief justice and five associates, all to be appointed by the president. On February 2, 1790, its first public session took place at the Royal Exchange in New York City, then the capital of the United States. In 1791 the capital and the Court moved to Philadelphia. However, the Supreme Court's first case was not decided until 1793. The Court went to Washington in 1800, when the District of Columbia became the nation's capital.

As the first president, George Washington appointed the first justices. Once named by a president and approved by the Senate, a justice can serve for life or as long as he or she is able to work. However, in the early years, few people wanted the job. Six justices should have attended the first session, but only four showed up. Many either turned down the offer or quit after a short time. One justice did not attend a single session for three years, then he resigned.

The first justices wore black robes with a red lining like English judges. They never put on the long, white wigs which are still used by British judges. With no permanent place to meet, the Supreme Court once even heard cases in a tavern.

John Jay was the first chief justice, serving from 1790 to 1795. When President George Washington asked his advice on a foreign policy matter, he refused to give it because the Court can decide only specific cases. Justice Jay resigned to become the governor of New York State. The second chief justice, John Rutledge, lasted only one year.

John Jay, the first chief justice of the United States. His long black robe is modeled on the robes worn by British justices.

Washington's third chief justice, Oliver Ellsworth, was chief justice in the four years from 1796 to 1800.

One reason no one wanted to be on the Supreme Court was that the judiciary law put each of the justices in charge of a district federal court. That meant they spent much of their time traveling back and forth. In those days roads were very rough, and such travel was a real hardship. Many of the men who were offered appointments thought they would be better off taking jobs in their home states. Under those conditions it is not surprising that in its first 12 years the Supreme Court heard only about five cases a year.

Another problem for the men who might become justices was that no one was quite sure what the Supreme

Court of the new United States of America was supposed to do. Could justices who were appointed by a president and served with the consent of the Senate really go against the wishes of either?

Alexander Hamilton thought that the power to decide if a law passed by a state or Congress fit in the rules of the Constitution belonged to the United States Supreme Court. However, both Thomas Jefferson and James Madison said that the states should decide for themselves whether laws they pass were constitutional.

This question came to a head after President John Adams named John Marshall to the Supreme Court in 1801. Two years later, a man named William Marbury brought a case to the Supreme Court that claimed that an act passed by the United States Congress was unconstitutional (went against the Constitution). The Supreme Court agreed. From that time on, everyone has accepted the fact that the Supreme Court has the right to decide what the wording of the Constitution means in certain situations. This ability to hold up other laws against what the Constitution means is called the power of judicial review.

Chief Justice Marshall believed that the Constitution gave the federal government great power over the states. He thought that without a strong federal government, the United States would not be a strong country. In 1810 the Court said that an act passed by a state was unconstitutional because it went against federal power. In 1819 the state of Maryland claimed that Congress had no right to establish the United States Bank. Chief Justice Marshall and other justices said it did. This case made it clear that federal power must win out over a state's powers when the two are at odds.

Even after the District of Columbia was created as the home of the federal government, the other two branches of government had buildings of their own long before the Supreme Court did. The president and his staff had the White House. The Senate and House of Representatives

John Marshall, the fourth chief justice of the United States. His decision in the 1803 William Marbury case established that the Supreme Court has the right to interpret the meaning of the Constitution.

met in the Capitol. But the Supreme Court moved into and out of several temporary quarters. In 1860 the Supreme Court took over the old Senate chamber in the U.S. Capitol. Twelve more rooms were used for the Court and its staff and records.

The justices were happy to have a robing room, a place where they could put on their long black robes. These robes, worn by nearly all judges, show that the individuals who wear them are aware of the authority of the law. Before then, their robes had hung from pegs on the wall, and the justices had to put them on in public.

Interior of the United States Capitol ca. 1851. The Supreme Court met there from 1860–1935.

Finally, in 1935, the Supreme Court got its very own building across a wide street from its old home in the United States Capitol. From the day it opened, it has been a favorite place for tourists to visit. One reason is that the Supreme Court Building is one of the most beautiful in Washington. The builders used the finest materials. It has so much marble that the building is nicknamed the Marble Palace. The building itself gives some idea of how important the serious work that takes place inside its walls is to the entire United States.

The Supreme Court building has the classical style of a Greek temple. This goes with the importance and dignity of the Court. At the base of the 36 steps leading to the entrance are two statues of large, seated figures. The one on the left is of a woman and is called Contemplation of Justice. Contemplation means thinking about justice, which is what the justices do. The one on the right shows a man as guardian or authority of law. This reminds everyone that the Supreme Court has the final power over the country's laws.

At the top of the steps, a double row of 24 columns supports a porch over huge bronze doors. Each door weighs six-and-a-half tons. On the doors are various scenes of lawgivers and lawmakers from the past. Overhead, the words "Equal Justice Under the Law" explain the purpose of the Supreme Court. It is up to the Court to make sure that all American citizens have the same rights, no matter how old or young or rich or poor they are.

Inside, still more tall marble columns line the Great Hall, which also has many statues of former chief justices. Twenty-four more columns surround the courtroom at the end of the Great Hall. Oak doors open into the courtroom, which is 82 feet by 91 feet. The ceiling in the courtroom is as high as a four-story building. More marble columns line this room, as well.

The building also contains offices, dining rooms, and even an exercise room for the nine justices and the more than 300 people who work for them. The Supreme Court library has over 450,000 law books, records, and journals.

In this stately building, the highest court in the land handles the many cases that come to it each year.

Attorney Johnnie Cochran (standing) defends his client, O. J. Simpson (seated, far right), during Simpson's 1995–1996 trial for murder. Even the most sensational criminal cases, such as Simpson's, can be tried in regular courts of law.

CHAPTER 2

What Courts Do

THE JUDICIAL BRANCH OF government settles all kind of disputes through courts of law. These courts make sure that everyone follows the rules of the land. They decide on the punishment for those who are found guilty of breaking laws. Another important job of the courts is to make sure that everyone gets all the rights guaranteed to them by the United States Constitution.

Disputes of law may be settled in several ways. At the local level, judges in special courts deal with simple kinds of everyday problems and disputes. For example, the place where you live probably has a traffic court for people accused of things like running red lights and speeding. A traffic court judge hears the facts and decides the outcome. Persons found to be guilty may have to pay a fine or perhaps go to a defensive driving school. In some cases they might even have to spend some time in jail.

Several other local courts also have one judge. Family courts handle divorce or child-custody cases. Small claims courts hear disputes between individuals or between an individual and a company that do not involve large amounts of money.

In America, persons under 18 years of age are considered to be minors or juveniles. A separate juvenile justice system deals with minors who break laws. Those who may be out of control or always in trouble at home and at school may be brought to juvenile court. When minors are ruled to be persons in need of supervision (or PINS), they can be brought to a juvenile detention center even if they have not been charged with a crime. The law states that minors, like adults, must get due process under the law. That means that all the rights set down in the Constitution and Bill of Rights must be followed.

Juvenile court judges decide in each case what will be done with those who appear before them. Sometimes minors are let go with probation, in which a court-appointed officer keeps in close touch with them. Some minors might be ordered to enroll in strict schools that are run like prisons. Others might be sent to boot camps that are like military basic training. The aim is to give them every chance to return to their homes and schools and help them stay out of trouble in the future. In the case of very serious crimes, minors can be tried as adults. This means that the case would go to a regular judge in the criminal court system.

Two kinds of cases may be brought to a regular court of law. In **criminal cases,** a crime has been committed or a law has been broken. These cases usually deal with serious crimes like murder, rape, theft, and selling or buying illegal drugs.

Civil cases deal with the private rights of individuals. They are brought by one person, or group, against another person or group. These people are known as parties, or sides, to the suit. Each case has two sides.

In a civil case the **plaintiff** brings a complaint or makes a charge that the **defendant** has caused damage to a person or to property. Sometimes the damage claimed is direct, such as if the plaintiff said the defendant caused the damage on purpose. For example, Mr. Jones might cut down a tree in Mr. Smith's yard because its leaves fell on the Jones's side of the property line.

In other civil cases the damage could be less direct, such as if a landlord allowed an unsafe condition, like trash in a hallway, that led the plaintiff to be hurt. This damage can be mental or emotional as well as physical. All civil cases ask the court to make the defendant give the plaintiff money in return for the damage claimed.

A courtroom during a trial, ca. 1940s. The judge is seated on his bench (left). The 12-person jury sits in the middle of the courtroom to the rear. An attorney stands in front of the jury addressing a witness.

All court cases take their names from the parties involved. In a criminal case, the state, as plaintiff, brings the charges against the accused, the defendant. For example, if a Mr. Smith in Maine is charged with a crime, the case will be known as *People of Maine v. Smith*. The *v.* stands for the Latin word versus, which means against. Sometimes versus is shown as *vs.*

A courtroom without a jury. Judges alone decide the outcome of cases in special courts at the local level, such as traffic, family, and small claims courts.

A state or local government might also be a party to a civil case. Mr. Smith's suit against Maine would be known as *Smith v. the State of Maine.* But if the state accuses Mr. Smith of doing something wrong, the suit would then be called *The State of Maine v. Smith.*

Some courts have both a judge and a jury. A jury is made up of people who live in the town or district in which cases are being tried. Most juries will have 12 people, although there may be fewer. The jury members sit in a special place in the courtroom and listen to the facts of a case. They then talk about it in private and make a decision about the case. Still other courts, including the United States Supreme Court, have several judges and no juries.

Higher than local courts are general trial courts. Every state divides its areas into judicial districts having one or more counties. Some have circuit courts made up of many districts. These trial courts deal with serious matters such as criminal cases and those involved with property and other rights. In most places those accused of a crime will have a trial before a petit, or regular, jury of 12 people. A grand jury is larger. Its usual job is to hear charges from the police officers and district attorney of the area and decide whether there is enough evidence to bring to court the cases that are presented. If the grand jury decides that the

Another type of special court is the television court, such as Judge Joseph A. Wapner's The People's Court. *Here small claims disputes between individuals are decided on the spot by the judge.*

answer is yes, these criminal and civil cases are decided by a trial before a jury and one judge.

Under the law, people are presumed (that is, supposed or thought) to be innocent unless facts prove beyond a "reasonable doubt" that they are guilty.

The party that brings a charge is called the prosecution. The party against whom the charge is made is known as the defendant. In most cases the **arguments** against the defendant are usually made by the local district attorney or someone from that office. The defense tries to show that the prosecution's charges are wrong or cannot be proved by the things presented as evidence.

When a case has been heard, the jury must decide which side is right. In a criminal case, if a jury finds that a defendant is guilty of the charges against him or her, it may tell the judge what punishment it thinks is appropriate. In courts with both a judge and jury, the jury decides the facts of a case. Then the judge decides how the laws apply to it. Either judge or jury may set a penalty. After being found guilty, a person may be sentenced to a certain period of time in prison.

Judges can change the jury's decision about the verdict or sentence in a case if they feel the decision made by the jury was not based on the facts brought out in the trial.

An early 1930s view of the new United States Supreme Court Building in Washington, D.C.

In a civil case, if the jury decides that the plaintiff is in the right, it has to say what the defendant must do as a result. Sometimes the defendant is ordered to pay money. A defendant might also have to return property or make things as right as possible.

If either party disagrees with the ruling of the general trial court, the party may **appeal.** Another court will be asked to change the first court's decision. The courts that deal with these kinds of cases are called **appellate courts.** In a state appellate court, judges look carefully at what happened with all the cases from the trial courts. They must see if the verdict was fair and if the original trial went as it should have. Most of the time their rulings are final. However, if the judges think some part of the trial might have raised a question about the state or federal constitution, the case can go on to the next level.

After the appellate courts, the next highest court is that state's supreme court. Here, as in the United States

Supreme Court, cases are heard by a chief justice and several other justices. The state supreme court has the final
word on the meaning of laws within the state. Its decisions
about the state constitution cannot be changed even by the
Supreme Court, unless a state law goes against the United
States Constitution.

If the state supreme court hears a case that brings up
questions about the United States Constitution, then it can
be sent on to the highest court in the land—the United
States Supreme Court.

Current Supreme Court justices. Chief Justice William Rehnquist is second from right.

CHAPTER **3**

How the Supreme Court Works

THE UNITED STATES COURTS of appeal were set up in 1891 to take the load off the United States Supreme Court. These courts do not have juries, and no facts can be presented. Appeals courts make sure that the lower courts did a good job in following legal rules. Other special federal courts of appeal handle matters of taxes, trade, military justice, and claims against the government. But even with the availability of these appellate courts, everyone seems to want to be heard by the United States Supreme Court.

Each year about 7,000 cases are presented to the Supreme Court. Most of these cases come from appellate **jurisdiction,** meaning they have come on appeal from the highest state courts or from lower federal courts.

Besides those that come directly to them at the Supreme Court, each of the nine justices, including the chief justice, has other cases. These come from the one or two federal circuits each justice takes care of. The justices may bring up cases from these districts on their own if they wish.

Under the Constitution the justices also have the right to deal directly with "all cases affecting Ambassadors, other public Ministers and Consuls, and those in which a State shall be a party." However, very few of these cases are brought each year.

The Supreme Court does not usually hear cases on appeal from a state supreme court. It takes such cases only when a state court makes some rule against an act of Congress or a treaty between the United States and another nation. Sometimes it takes a case when someone claims that a state supreme court ruling has gone against rights guaranteed by the federal Constitution.

Although the Supreme Court is asked to review several thousand cases each year, only a few hundred are picked to be heard. First, the persons bringing the case must show that they have been hurt or will be better off if the court overthrows, or changes the decision of a lower court. Second, the court must be willing and able to take the needed action. Sometimes the Supreme Court says that it does not have jurisdiction, meaning the right to hear the case.

The Court usually takes cases where its ruling will affect the entire country, rather than only a few people. At least four justices must agree that a case is really important. Then it is put on the list for review. Only some 160 to 200 of the thousands of cases sent to the Court get that far. From them, the Supreme Court puts out around 80 signed decisions each year.

A term of the Supreme Court always begins on the first Monday in October. For two weeks the justices will hear cases during sittings. Then in two weeks of recess, they decide on what they heard in the sittings. This cycle of sittings and recesses continues through May. Each term lasts until late June or early July. The Court recesses at the end of June, but the justices work all summer to get ready for the next term.

When they are hearing cases, the justices begin work at 9:30 A.M. on most days. They meet all day in the conference room to pick new cases for the Court to review. They also vote on the cases they have already heard during the past week. This meeting is so secret that no one else knows what any of the justices said about those cases.

Once a case is chosen for review by the Supreme Court, the lawyers on both sides submit a **brief,** a written summary of facts or reasons they used in preparing the case. Then the justices listen as the lawyers for each side give oral (spoken) arguments in the large Courtroom. Usually all nine justices are present. However, a case may be heard by as few as six.

When the Court is in session, it begins at 10:00 A.M. Everyone stands as a sign of respect when the marshal calls out, "The honorable, the chief justice and the associate justices of the Supreme Court of the United States. Oyez! Oyez! Oyez!"

The robed justices then enter the room and sit at a long table (the bench) in a sort of half-circle. The chief justice is in the middle. The other justices take their places according to how long they have been members of the Supreme Court. The ones who have been there the longest

United States Supreme Court chambers. The nine justices sit at the bench directly in front of the pillars, with the chief justice seated in the middle.

sit closer to the chief justice. Each justice shakes hands with every other justice at the start of every session.

The lawyers arguing cases before the Court sit at tables in front of the bench. For a long time lawyers who came to the Supreme Court dressed up. They wore the kind of long, formal black coats you might see today at a wedding. Now, only the Department of Justice and other government lawyers wear formal dress. One old custom goes back to the start of the Court—white quill pens are still put on all the Courtroom tables.

When it is their turn, the lawyers speak from a stand in the center, facing the justices. Behind them, seats are reserved for the press and special guests of the justices.

One part of the large courtroom is set aside for the public. People touring the building may come in and listen quietly for a few moments. They can also register to be present for the morning session (10:00 A.M. to 12:00 noon) or the afternoon session (1:00 P.M. to 3:00 P.M.). Once they are seated, these visitors must stay until the session is over.

Since the Court may hear up to 22 to 24 cases a day, each side has only 30 minutes to present its case. There is no jury, and no witnesses are heard. The Court has already studied what happened when the case went through lower courts. It has also read the printed arguments of each side. The justices usually ask the lawyers questions and listen carefully to their answers.

After the public hearing of the cases, the justices meet again in private. They talk about how they think the law should apply to each case. Many of the decisions are made the same week that the cases are heard. Sometimes the cases are so hard to decide that it takes many weeks, or even months, for the justices to reach their decision.

When all the justices have had a chance to talk about their ideas on a case, they vote on how they think it should be settled. A yes vote means that they think that the past ruling made in the case was wrong. Cases are decided on a majority vote. That means that at least five of the nine justices have to vote the same way to change the ruling of a lower court.

When the chief justice votes yes on the question, he usually asks one of the justices who agrees with him to write the majority **opinion.** An opinion is a formal statement of the court's reasons for its decisions. Any justice may write a concurring, or agreeing, opinion. Any justices who do not agree with the vote of the majority may write a dissenting opinion. A dissenting opinion explains their reasons for disagreeing with the majority decision.

On the days when the Court is ready to let everyone know how it has ruled, the justices read their decisions. They also give out printed copies of these decisions. About half of the Court's cases are decided and made public by May. The rest are announced in June and early July.

Rulings that make important points that might change the way people look at the law are called **precedents.** Once the Court has made a ruling in a case and put its reasons in writing, these papers become an important guide for others who might want to bring cases like it to the Supreme Court in the future. Lawyers study rulings to see how the Court answered the many questions that came before it. Doing so helps them prepare future cases.

The Court term officially ends in June. At that time Court is in recess, but that does not mean that the Justices have nothing to do until the first Monday in October. Supreme Court justices work all summer. They look at new appeals and prepare for the cases they will hear when the next term begins.

Supreme Court justices do not have an easy job, but the work they do is very important. Every American should thank them for trying to make sure that our laws are fair and that we do have "justice for all."

*Supreme Court Justice
Thurgood Marshall became the
first African American to join
the Court in 1967.*

CHAPTER **4**

Famous Supreme Court Justices

THE UNITED STATES CONSTITUTION calls for a Supreme Court headed by a chief justice. The president of the United States has the job of picking people for the Court. The Senate can confirm, or accept, them. It can also reject, or turn down, the president's choices. Since 1789 the Senate has turned down almost one out of five of the names sent to it.

The Constitution made no rules about Supreme Court justices. Nothing says that a justice must ever have been a judge. A justice does not even have to be a lawyer. Still, presidents have usually chosen people who have been lawyers and who know a lot about the law. The Senate would not likely agree to let anyone serve on the Supreme Court who could not do the work.

Since they have their jobs for life, about half of all the justices have died while still in office. Others quit when they got too old or sick to do their work. About every two years, a justice has to be

Franklin D. Roosevelt is sworn into office as president by Chief Justice of the United States Charles Evans Hughes on March 4, 1933. Hughes, at age 68, was the oldest chief justice ever appointed.

replaced. Nearly every president since George Washington has had the chance to send at least one name to the Senate for the Supreme Court. President Franklin D. Roosevelt holds the record for placing the most justices on the Supreme Court. Between 1937 and 1943, President Roosevelt appointed eight men to the Supreme Court. He also made Harlan Stone, an associate justice, the chief justice.

Presidents usually pick people for the Supreme Court who think the same way they do. Each president hopes that the justice's rulings will go the way the president wants them to go. Once in office, a justice can sometimes surprise the president who put him or her there. For example, President Theodore Roosevelt did not agree with some of the things that Oliver Wendell Holmes Jr. did. "That man has the backbone of a banana," President Roosevelt once complained.

The first important Supreme Court justice was the fourth one, John Marshall. He was appointed to the Supreme Court by President John Adams and served from 1801 until 1835. Under Chief Justice Marshall, the

Supreme Court for the first time became the powerful third branch of the government the Constitution called for.

Under Marshall, several cases proved this power. In *Marbury v. Madison* in 1803, the Supreme Court made it clear that it alone had the right to decide what the words in the Constitution meant. In *Fletcher v. Peck* in 1810, Marshall led the Court to say that an act passed by a state was unconstitutional because it went against federal power. In *McCulloch v. Maryland* in 1819, the Court ruled that Congress had the power to make a United States Bank.

Chief Justice Marshall was the first to get the other judges to join him in writing down their opinions and the reasons for them. Judges who did not agree on the ruling could still write separate opinions, but the majority opinion would speak for the Court. This same process is still used today.

In Marshall's last 24 years as chief justice, many of the justices who served on the Supreme Court opposed his belief in a strong central government. He was able to present his ideas in such a clear way that the other justices often voted with him instead of against him. While he was chief justice, the Supreme Court made over 1,100 decisions. Of these, Marshall wrote the majority opinion on more than 500. Even today, many legal questions and Supreme Court decisions go back to John Marshall's rulings.

Joseph Story came to the Supreme Court as an associate justice in 1812 and served until his death in 1845. When he arrived he was only 28 years old, the youngest person ever to be on the Supreme Court. Even before that, Justice Story had served in Congress. Starting in 1829, he also taught law at Harvard University. He joined with Chief Justice Marshall in making important rulings. What he wrote about American common law is still studied today.

It took more than one try before the Senate finally let Roger Taney (TAWN-eh) serve on the Supreme Court in

Roger Taney, chief justice of the United States. His Dred Scott decision of 1857 said that a slave who had lived in free territory for many years had no rights as a United States citizen and no right to sue in a federal court.

1836. He had been a state senator in Maryland before President Andrew Jackson made him the attorney general of the United States in 1831. President Jackson was against the United States Bank. In 1833 he tried to name Taney secretary of the treasury, so he could take the government's money out of the bank. That made Congress so mad that they would not agree to let Taney serve in that office.

In 1835 Jackson tried to make Taney an associate justice of the Supreme Court. The Senate turned him down again. Finally, in 1836, a new group of senators approved Jackson's appointment of Taney.

Taney favored the rights of states but not over basic national powers. He took part in many rulings, but he is

best known for the so-called Dred Scott decision of 1857. The ruling in that case played a large part in leading the country into civil war only a few years later.

Oliver Wendell Holmes Jr., who was an associate justice from 1902 until 1932, was 90 years old when he finally retired. As a Union soldier in the Civil War, he was wounded three times. Once he saw a tall man standing near a battlefield and yelled at him to get down. Later, he discovered that the man was President Abraham Lincoln.

Chief Justice Holmes disagreed so often with the opinions of others on the Court that he got the nickname, the Great Dissenter. In his later years, as new justices came to the Court, he saw some of his original dissents become the majority opinion.

Oliver Wendell Holmes Jr. as a Union officer during the Civil War. As chief justice, Holmes was called the Great Dissenter because he frequently disagreed with the opinions of other Supreme Court justices.

Holmes once said of the Supreme Court, "It is quiet here, but it is the quiet of a storm center."

In 1916, with the consent of the Senate, President Woodrow Wilson named Louis D. Brandeis to be an asso-

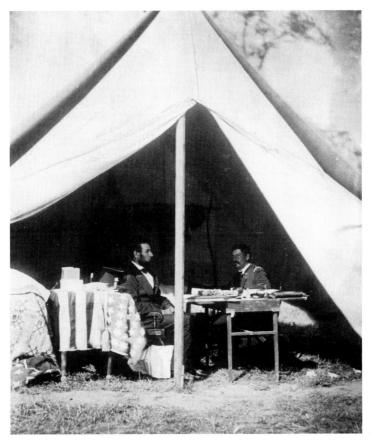

President Abraham Lincoln, shown here with Union General George B. McClellan (right) after the 1862 Battle of Antietam, liked to visit the army when possible to encourage the soldiers. Future Chief Justice Oliver Wendell Holmes Jr., not recognizing the president as he stood near a battlefield, once shouted at him to get under cover.

ciate justice. This first Jewish justice continued to serve for 20 years. He took part in many important rulings on civil rights and other questions of liberty.

Just as Joseph Story was the youngest to become a justice, Charles Evan Hughes was the oldest man ever to become the chief justice. He was an associate justice from 1910 until 1916. He resigned to run for president of the United States as a Republican against Democrat Woodrow Wilson. Hughes was 68 years old in 1930 when President Herbert Hoover named him chief justice of the Supreme Court. He stayed on as chief justice for 11 more years. During that time he made many rulings for personal freedoms.

When William Howard Taft became the chief justice of the Supreme Court in 1921, he was also the first and

Louis D. Brandeis, the first Jewish justice to serve on the Supreme Court. He made many important decisions on civil rights and liberty.

only person to be both president and a Supreme Court justice. As president, Taft had appointed William White chief justice in 1910. The next chief justice was Taft himself, appointed by President Herbert Hoover.

A very important first for the Supreme Court happened in 1967, when Thurgood Marshall became the first African American to join the Court.

As a group, the Supreme Court justices are called the Brethren, or the Brothers. Until 1981 this name fit because they were all men. However, that year Sandra Day O'Connor became the first woman to be named an associate jus-

William Howard Taft was the only person to have occupied the positions of both president of the United States and Supreme Court justice.

Sandra Day O'Connor, the first woman to be named a Supreme Court justice. Serving as associate justice since 1981, she was joined by the second female justice, Ruth Bader Ginsburg, in 1993.

tice. She is still serving, as is Ruth Bader Ginsburg, who became the second female associate justice in 1993.

Whatever their background, age, or sex, these justices all have one thing in common: each has had to decide how to rule on many very important cases.

CHAPTER 5

Famous Cases and Decisions

MOST OF THE WORK of the Supreme Court passes with little notice. Many of its cases deal with very complex matters. Some of the Court's rulings are hard for anyone who is not a lawyer to understand. Other decisions, such as which of two states may use water from a river that flows through both, mean very little to the average person. But over the years, many Supreme Court decisions have changed Americans' lives. These cases have stood out because of their interest to everyone.

Just as occurs in lower courts, the cases that reach the Supreme Court are known by the names of the person or people bringing them (the plaintiff) and those the case is brought against (the defendant). In the case called *Schenck v. United States,* the Supreme Court had to decide on a matter of freedom of speech.

Many World War I soldiers had been drafted into the military. Charles Schenck, a Socialist jailed for trying to keep men from obeying the draft, appealed his sentence, saying his right to free speech had been violated. The Supreme Court ruled that the government can deny free speech when the nation and its people are in danger.

Schenck v. United States

In 1917 the United States entered World War I against Germany and other European countries. To make sure that there would be enough soldiers to defend the United States, Congress passed a law that said all young men should register for possible army service. If they were then drafted (asked to serve), they would have to agree to join the army or risk being put in jail.

In the same year Congress also passed the Espionage Act. (Espionage is the word that spy comes from.) Part of this act made it against the law for anyone to try to keep people from serving in the armed forces.

A group called the United States Socialist Party did not think that America should be in the war. They claimed that the draft was unconstitutional. Members of the Socialist Party printed leaflets that asked those who had been drafted not to allow themselves to be taken into the army. The leaflets also asked people to work to do away with the draft law.

Charles Schenck was a Socialist Party leader in the office where the leaflets were handed out. He was charged in federal court under the Espionage Act for trying to keep men from joining the army. He was sentenced to six months in jail. Schenck then appealed the ruling, saying it violated his free speech rights. He pointed to the First Amendment to the United States Constitution, which says that Congress shall make no law to take away an American's right to free speech.

Before the Supreme Court took this case, it had never been asked to consider a case about freedom of speech. It could have ruled in several ways.

First, it could have agreed with Schenck and said that the Espionage Act was unconstitutional. In that case Schenck would have won.

Second, it could have agreed with the lower court. The Espionage Act would have stood, and Schenck would have had to spend time in jail.

Third, it could have let the Espionage Act stand but have allowed Schenck to go free.

The Court agreed that the United States has the right to deny free speech when the country and its people are in danger. This is like saying that no one has the "right" to yell "Fire!" in a crowded theater when there is not a fire. A person's right to free speech ends when what he or she says becomes a danger to others. The government also has the right to protect its citizens by stopping anything that might cause harm to the nation in a time of war.

In this case, the court said that the general good of all American citizens was more important than Mr. Schenck's right to free speech. Ever since this decision, if something is "a clear and present danger" to the country, then an individual or the press does not have the right to say or do it, since it could harm America or its people.

Barnette v. Board of Education

Another case that had to do with the First Amendment right to free speech started in 1942. That year, the West Virginia Board of Education ordered that all public schools in the state must make a salute to the United States flag "a regular part of school activities." Students who did not salute the flag would be expelled from school or counted absent for the day without an excuse. At worst, the law said such students could be sent to reform schools for juveniles. The parents of these students could be fined and sent to jail.

This law was meant to help all students show their respect for their country. But for a group of Jehovah's Witnesses, a religious denomination, saluting the flag was against their beliefs. When they refused to join in the salute, Jehovah's Witnesses children were expelled from several schools. Three of their parents, including Walter Barnette, brought suit in federal district court. They said that the law went against both their religious freedom and right to free speech.

A federal district court agreed with the parents and ordered that the law requiring a flag salute should not be enforced. The West Virginia Board of Education then appealed the decision to the Supreme Court, where it was called *Barnette v. Board of Education.*

The Supreme Court announced its decision on Flag Day, June 14, 1943. Six of its nine members voted that state and local governments could not require anyone to salute the flag or say a pledge of allegiance to the United States. Many people disagreed with the Court's decision and continued to have flag salutes and the pledge of allegiance in public places. However, in those places, persons could not be punished if they did not take part.

This ruling made it clear that the Bill of Rights would continue to be protected by the Supreme Court.

Gideon v. Wainwright

Most cases come to the Supreme Court through lower courts, but a man named Clarence Gideon got a hearing from a letter he wrote to the Supreme Court in April 1962.

Clarence Gideon was arrested for a robbery and was tried in Florida in 1961. When he came to court, Gideon told the judge that he had no lawyer. He asked the court to appoint someone to represent him during the trial. The judge said he could not do as Mr. Gideon asked. Under Florida law, a court could give a defendant a free lawyer only if the person faced a possible death sentence.

Gideon acted as his own lawyer and called his own witnesses. A jury found him guilty of the charge of "breaking and entering," and sentenced him to prison. Gideon

In 1942, the West Virginia Board of Education ordered that all public school students must salute the flag. Members of the Jehovah's Witnesses brought suit against the board, saying that this was against their beliefs. The Supreme Court's decision was that no one could be forced under law to salute the flag or say a pledge of allegiance to the United States.

still believed that he had a constitutional right to have a lawyer.

In April 1962 he wrote a letter to the Supreme Court. He had studied law books in prison and followed the formal rules of an appeal. He named Louie Wainwright, the director of Florida's Division of Corrections, as the defendant.

The Supreme Court had had a case 20 years earlier in which it ruled six to three not to make states furnish lawyers for defendants unless they were facing a possible death sentence. Since then, all but 13 states, including Florida, had given the right to have a court-appointed lawyer to all defendants. The question Gideon had raised made the justices decide if it was fair for some states to give poor people a lawyer, while others did not.

The Court's decision came on March 19, 1963. All of the nine justices agreed that every defendant accused of a crime should have a lawyer. Justice Hugo Black wrote, "there can be no equal justice where the kind of trial a man gets depends on the amount of money he has."

The Supreme Court gave Clarence Gideon a new trial and appointed a lawyer to defend him. This time the jury did not find Gideon guilty of the charges brought against him.

The Gideon decision does not guarantee that poor people will have lawyers that are as competent as those that rich people have. It does, however, give poor people the right to have a lawyer. It also shows that even someone like Clarence Gideon can get a hearing before the Supreme Court.

Miranda v. Arizona

In March 1963 a man named Ernesto Miranda was arrested in Phoenix, Arizona. He was put into a lineup with three other Hispanic men. Police asked him questions with no lawyer being present for two hours. After being told that a woman had said he was the one who had hurt her, Miranda signed a confession that said he did the crime. The confession had a printed part that said that Miranda had confessed of his own free will and with full knowledge of his legal rights.

When the case came to trial, Miranda changed his story. He said he did not commit the crime to which he had confessed. He also said that no one had told him of his legal rights. The trial judge allowed the prosecution to show the confession. A jury found Miranda guilty of the charges against him and sentenced him to two long prison terms.

From prison Miranda appealed his case to the Arizona Supreme Court. He said his constitutional rights had been taken away because he did not have a lawyer before he was questioned. He also said he did not know that what he said could be used against him in a court of law.

When the Arizona Supreme Court upheld Miranda's conviction, he appealed to the United States Supreme Court.

Here, the Supreme Court had to consider the meaning of the Fifth Amendment to the U.S. Constitution. It states that "No person . . . shall be compelled in any criminal case to be a witness against himself, nor be deprived of life, liberty, or property, without **due process of law.**"

In other words, a citizen does not have to admit things he or she may have done. No one can have his life taken, be put into jail, or have what he owns taken until all legal steps have been properly made.

Miranda also claimed that the police did not give him his Sixth Amendment right to "the assistance of counsel [a lawyer] for his defense."

After studying the case, the justices ruled five to four in agreement with Miranda. They said that his confession could not be presented as evidence and that police must let

Chief Justice Earl Warren (seated, third from left) defined the four items police must tell a crime suspect about his or her rights prior to questioning.

defendants know their constitutional rights before they question them.

This decision was not popular, and justices on both sides tried to explain the reasons for the way they voted. Chief Justice Earl Warren knew that police held great power over prisoners being questioned. As a former district attorney, he knew that police sometimes confused defendants about what their rights were.

To make these rights clear, Warren made some rules. Before asking questions of a suspect in a crime, police must tell them the following:

1. They have a right to remain silent.
2. Anything they say can be used against them in a court of law.
3. They have the right to have an attorney present during questioning.
4. If they cannot afford a lawyer, the court will appoint one for them before questioning.

Today, police officers carry cards with this information printed on them. They make sure to "read their rights" at the time a person is arrested.

The decisions made by the Supreme Court in these cases all caused changes in the way people might think or act at certain times. The cases are different, yet they all have to do in some way with Americans' individual rights and freedoms.

Some Supreme Court rulings, such as the 1973 Roe v. Wade decision, continue to upset many people. Here pro-life protesters stand in front of the Supreme Court Building on the 23rd anniversary of its decision to uphold a woman's right to have an abortion over a state's right to pass its own laws.

CHAPTER 6

How the Court Overrules Itself

WE HAVE LEARNED THAT the rulings of the Supreme Court become guides for the way laws will be carried out. The Supreme Court also decides on what the words in the United States Constitution mean. We have seen that decisions made by the earliest Supreme Courts still stand. For those reasons, you might think that the Supreme Court never changes its mind about matters that come before it. But times and ideas about what is right sometimes change. Remember, the Constitution is a living document, and some decisions made by Supreme Courts in the past have been changed, or overruled, by later Courts.

One of the best examples of how the outcome of a case can change is the Dred Scott decision, which was mentioned earlier.

In 1857 the Supreme Court heard a case called *Dred Scott v. Sandford.* Dred Scott was the slave of a Missouri army surgeon named John Emerson. In 1834 the doctor took Scott to the free state of Illinois, where slavery was against the law. Then he went to the land that became the state of Wisconsin. By a law known as the Missouri Compromise, this state also could not allow slavery. In 1838 Scott's master took him back to the slave state of Missouri. When Emerson died, Scott was sold to John Sanford (his name is misspelled in the reports).

Scott had been told that when he was moved to a free state, he had become a free man. In 1846 he went to court to ask for his freedom. The state circuit court agreed with him. Sanford then appealed the case to the Missouri Supreme Court, which ruled against him. Because Scott had lived in more than one state, the case was then sent to a federal court. From there it made its way to the United States Supreme Court.

Its ruling, the Dred Scott decision, has been called one of the worst any Supreme Court ever made. In it the Supreme Court said that it had no jurisdiction over the case—that is, it had no right to say that Scott was made free just by living in a free state. He was still a slave, and a slave was not a citizen. Only a citizen could bring a case to federal court.

When Chief Justice Roger Taney announced the Court's decision on March 6, 1857, many people did not agree. They thought the Supreme Court was wrong. The Dred Scott decision made things even worse between the North and the South. It is often given as one of the causes of the Civil War, which started only four years later.

In 1863, during that war, President Abraham Lincoln made public a paper called the Emancipation Proclamation, ordering that slaves in the Confederate states were to be freed. (To emancipate means to free. To proclaim means to tell.)

In 1865, the same year that the Civil War was over, the 13th Amendment to the Constitution of the United States officially ended slavery. One year later the 14th Amendment was added to the Constitution. It said that all persons

One of the measures segregating African Americans in the Supreme Court's 1896 Plessy v. Ferguson decision said that they must occupy separate waiting rooms in public transportation stations. It was still being enforced in this Jackson, Mississippi, bus station in 1961.

(including former slaves) born in the United States were citizens. Everyone had the same rights.

Although the amendment had passed, not everyone agreed with it. As a result, a case called *Plessy v. Ferguson* came to the Supreme Court in 1896. This case upheld an 1890 Louisiana law that made railroads provide "separate but equal accommodations for the white and colored races." This law segregated (set apart) black people in waiting rooms in train stations. They had to ride in a different railroad car than white people. Nonwhites were also made to drink from a different water fountain. They could not even enter some places, which were set aside for "white only."

When it ruled in this case, the Supreme Court said that state laws that separated the races were all right as long as nonwhites had the same kinds of things as the whites. This is known as "separate but equal."

Many states continued the "separate" part of the ruling, while ignoring the "equal" part. In a case concerning schools brought in 1899, the Supreme Court refused to make Augusta, Georgia, close its high schools for whites until it reopened a school for nonwhites.

Then in 1954 the Supreme Court chose a case from Topeka, Kansas, for review. The laws of Kansas said that any city with more than 15,000 people could choose to integrate their schools (have both races attend the same schools) or provide "separate but equal" schools for nonwhite students. The city of Topeka chose to have nonwhites and whites in different schools.

In 1950, 13 parents, including a man named Oliver Brown, tried to enroll their children in schools set aside for white students only. When the Topeka School Board turned them down, the parents appealed their case until it finally reached the Supreme Court. This time, all nine Supreme Court justices agreed that separating school students by race went against the nonwhite children's constitutional rights to equal protection under the law.

Although this ruling made desegregation the law of the land, it did not happen quickly. The Court's ruling called for integration to be done "with all deliberate speed." Some local and state school boards thought that meant that they had many years to put the races together in the same schools. In some cases federal judges ordered schools to provide ways to carry out the Supreme Court's ruling.

Since 1954, cases from all over the United States have tested the ruling and some of the ways that school districts have tried to deal with it.

In 1964 Congress passed the Civil Rights Act to make sure that everyone got all the rights called for in the 14th Amendment. The Supreme Court agreed that Congress had the power to create those laws. But many people thought that passing a bill then did nothing to undo the damage that had already been done. In 1965 President Lyndon Johnson used his power as the chief executive to order universities and business owners to give more jobs to nonwhites and women. This type of policy was called Affirmative Action.

Although it became law in 1954, desegregation did not happen quickly. Three years later, African-American students needed the help of United States Army troops to safely enter their high school in Little Rock, Arkansas.

As a result, the University of California at Davis decided to accept fewer whites. When a white man named Allan Bakke was not allowed to enroll in medical school there, he took the case to a federal court. He said that the Davis policy was against the rights he should have under the 14th Amendment. The case went to the California Supreme Court in 1976. That court agreed with Bakke and ordered the school to let him in. Then the University of California appealed to the U.S. Supreme Court to say that the state Supreme Court's ruling had been wrong. The case was called *Regents of the University of California v. Bakke.*

In one of its strangest rulings, the Court upheld the California Supreme Court's decision that Bakke must be let in the school. But it did not say that Affirmative Action programs were wrong. Everyone on the Court seemed to have a different idea about what, if anything, should be done to make sure that everyone had the same chances.

Chief Justice Lewis Powell wrote that it was good to try to fix mistakes from the past, but that legally it was not possible. He said that people living now could not possibly reach back into history and take care of all the injustices done to nonwhites and other minorities in the past. The next year the Court let employers set up their own Affirmative Action programs.

Over the years many cases have come to the Supreme Court that tested ways a school system used to carry out its order. In a 1971 case called *Swann v. Charlotte-Mecklenburg Board of Education,* the Court approved several ways. These included busing students from one area to another and changing school zone lines. As it has done in past cases, the Supreme Court left room for future justices to decide whether or not these programs should continue.

Some people have used the words of the Ninth Amendment to the Constitution to prove that they are right. The Ninth Amendment says that citizens' rights are not limited to those that the Constitution sets forth. Many then added the words of the Fourteenth Amendment to the Ninth Amendment and said it applied to all state and federal laws. In other words a court *could* allow an individual to go against a state law if the law went against the individual's rights.

Some cases have raised questions about whether individuals are allowed, under the laws of the Constitution, to do certain things. The Supreme Court's rulings have caused many people to think about what should be done.

A case that is still widely discussed is known as *Roe v. Wade,* which began with a Texas case. A woman who took the alias Jane Roe brought a case against Henry Wade, a prosecuting attorney in Dallas County, Texas.

A law passed in Texas in 1854 said that a woman could not have an abortion (terminate a pregnancy) unless doing so would save her life. By 1910 all but one state had similar laws. In time, however, many states changed their laws to make abortion possible. Texas did not change its law, and the *Roe v. Wade* case was brought to do just that.

The district court said that the state of Texas had not been shown that it had any reason to change the law. It said that the 10th Amendment gives states the right to pass their own laws.

The Supreme Court had a hard time deciding this case. Their decision to strike down the Texas law was finally announced on January 22, 1973. Chief Justice Harry Blackmun said that the Constitution protects a person's right to privacy. The majority of the justices decided that this gives a woman the right to choose to have an abortion.

Like the rulings on Dred Scott and *Brown v. Board of Education,* this Supreme Court decision upset a great many people. Although many presidents and lawmakers thought the Court's decision in *Roe v. Wade* was wrong, many other people supported it. The Court ruling is still in force. If a future Supreme Court decides to take a case testing the *Roe v. Wade* decision, those justices could overturn it.

The only other way to change a Court ruling is to amend the Constitution. We have seen how that was done in cases involving outlawing slavery and providing civil rights. Adding amendments to the Constitution is not easy. The founders of the nation said that any amendment to the Constitution must first be approved by a two-thirds vote of both houses of Congress. It becomes a law only when passed by three-fourths of the states. In the more than two centuries since the Constitution was first written, only 26 amendments have been added to it.

The Supreme Court may sometimes be thought of as a less important part of the United States government than are the president and Congress. Yet, without the many decisions made by the Supreme Court justices over the years, our country might be quite different today.

Many of the cases that come to the Supreme Court do not sound very interesting. Some rulings go into points of law that are hard for the average person to understand. The decisions of the Supreme Court, however, often change the lives of every man, woman, and child in this country. Remember that the next time you hear or see news about the Supreme Court.

In its job of protecting our freedom and seeing that our laws are fair and just, the Supreme Court helps all of us to make the most of being American citizens.

Glossary

Appeal—A request for a decision made by a court of law to be changed.

Appellate court—A court that hears cases appealed from a lower court.

Argument—A point of view or reason.

Brief—A summary of facts or arguments to be used by a lawyer in preparing a court case.

Civil case—A case that deals with the private rights of individuals.

Criminal case—A case in which a crime has been committed or a law has been broken.

Defendant—The person in a court case who has been accused of doing something wrong or who is being sued.

Due process of law—A guarantee that fair and regular rights and procedures are accorded to those who come before a court.

Jurisdiction—The power of a court to hear and decide a case based in its authority over the parties.

Opinion—The judgment of the Supreme Court or of individual justices, formed after careful thought.

Plaintiff—A person who brings a complaint against a defendant to court in a lawsuit.

Precedent—A legal decision that may serve as an example for later cases.

Further Reading

Aria, Barbara. *The Supreme Court.* New York: Franklin Watts, 1994.

Friedman, Leon. *The Supreme Court.* New York: Chelsea House, 1987.

Kronenwetter, Michael. *The Supreme Court of the United States.* Springfield, NJ: Enslow Publishers, 1996.

Patrick, John J. *The Young Oxford Companion to the Supreme Court of the United States.* New York: Oxford University Press, 1993.

Stein, R. Conrad. *The Story of the Powers of the Supreme Court.* Chicago: Children's Press, 1989.

Stein, Sharman. "How Did the Court Rule? Now You Decide." *Junior Scholastic,* January 11, 1999, pp. 8–10.

"Supreme Court Further Defines Teenagers' Rights." *Christian Science Monitor,* March 23, 1999, p. 4.

Witt, Elder, ed. *The Supreme Court A to Z.* Washington, D.C.: Congressional Quarterly, 1993.

Index

ABOUT THE AUTHOR: Former English teacher Kay Cornelius is a full-time freelance writer who lives in Huntsville, Alabama. She likes to study and write about history. She has written magazine articles, short stories, one novella, and nine novels, most about history. *The Supreme Court* is her first children's book.

SENIOR CONSULTING EDITOR Arthur M. Schlesinger, jr. is the leading American historian of our time. He won the Pulitzer Prize for his book *The Age of Jackson* (1945) and again for *A Thousand Days* (1965). This chronicle of the Kennedy Administration also won a National Book Award. Professor Schlesinger is the Albert Schweitzer Professor of the Humanities at the City University of New York, and has been involved in several other Chelsea House projects, including the REVOLUTIONARY WAR LEADERS and COLONIAL LEADERS series.

Picture Credits